HAVE YOU EVER HEARD
OF A KANGAROO BIRD?

HAVE YOU EVER HEARD OF A KANGAROO BIRD?

Fascinating Facts
About Unusual Birds

BY BARBARA BRENNER
ILLUSTRATED BY IRENE BRADY

Coward, McCann & Geoghegan, Inc.
New York

My thanks to Mr. John Bull of the American Museum of Natural History for his reading and valuable comments on this book.

Text copyright © 1980 by Barbara Brenner
Illustrations copyright © 1980 by Irene Brady
All rights reserved. This book, or parts thereof,
may not be reproduced in any form without permission
in writing from the publishers. Published simultaneously
in Canada by Academic Press Canada Limited, Toronto
(formerly Longman Canada Limited).

LIBRARY OF CONGRESS CATALOGING IN PUBLICATION DATA
Brenner, Barbara
Have you ever heard of a kangaroo bird?
Includes index.
Summary: Presents facts about unusual birds
including the brightly colored puffin, the California
condor, and an accomplished builder, the bowerbird.
1. Birds–Miscellanea–Juvenile literature.
[1. Birds–Miscellanea] I. Brady, Irene.
II. Title.
QL676.2.B73   598.2   79-14707
ISBN 0-698-20446-8

First printing
Printed in the United States of America

Contents

This book is about some of the most unusual birds in the world. In it you'll find out *why* they look so peculiar and why they do what they do.

The *tailorbird* of tropical Asia gets its name from the fact that it actually sews together its nest of leaves, using plant fibers for thread. The tailorbird can even make knots!

You might call the *hoopoe* the skunk of the bird world. This bird of Europe, Asia and Africa protects its young by releasing a horrible-smelling fluid from a gland at the base of its tail.

The *chimney swift,* which makes its nest in chimneys, is a super flier that seldom lands except when nesting; it eats, sleeps, bathes and even mates on the wing.

A tropical bird called the *finfoot* has been nicknamed the *kangaroo bird.* As you can see in the frontispiece, the male carries the young in pockets under its wings.

The *Egyptian vulture* gets to its favorite dinner of ostrich egg by cracking the egg with a stone. These birds have been seen throwing rocks weighing as much as two pounds.

The long-necked water-turkey, or *snakebird,* of the tropics has a beak shaped like a spear. That's the way it uses the beak—diving under the water to spear a fish for food.

And there's more . . .

1/ Is That a Flying Dinosaur?

Try to imagine a day about 140 million years ago, before there were people. In the swamps a brontosaurus is browsing. On land, a tyrannosaurus chases its prey and a pterodactyl is flying overhead. Suddenly a creature about the size of a crow half hops, half flies down a rocky ledge. What is it? A lizard with wings? A flying dinosaur? It is neither. It is a bird, *archaeopteryx*.

Archaeopteryx is the oldest bird we know of. Its fossil remains were discovered in 1861, and from them experts have put together a model of what archaeopteryx probably looked like.

It was a very strange-looking creature—more reptile than bird. Its head was shaped like that of a lizard. It still had teeth like a reptile and the fingers and claws of a reptile on its wings. Archaeopteryx probably didn't fly very well. But then, archaeopteryx was only the *first* bird. Bird design was going to change a lot over millions of years. Still, there was something new about this creature. Feathers. And it is feathers that make a bird.

All birds of today look a little bit like this first bird. There is even one bird, the *hoatzin* (p. 40), whose young have claws on their wings, like archaeopteryx.

2/ How Does the Oilbird See in the Dark?

It is dusk. From a cave on the island of Trinidad come eerie, piercing screams. "The murderers are crying out," say the people of this Caribbean island. "Their souls are in the bodies of the *guacharos*."

As night falls, the guacharos, or *oilbirds*, stream out of the cave by the hundreds. Their eyes gleam red in the darkness, making them look like creatures from a ghost story.

But the real story of the oilbirds is more fantastic than any tall tale you could make up. They are among the few birds that travel by using sonar, or echolocation. During the day, the oilbirds roost on rock ledges deep inside caves. They are in almost total darkness, yet they have no trouble finding their way. As they fly, they make rapid clicking sounds, sometimes as many as three hundred in one second. By listening to the echoes of their own sounds, the oilbirds can tell how far they are from the sides of the cave walls and from one another.

Oilbirds travel great distances each night, some-

times as much as 50 miles, in their search for food. Their main diet is the fruit of the palm, which makes their flesh oily and gives the birds their name.

Unfortunately for the oilbirds, this fat is very fine for cooking. For that reason, the flesh of the oilbirds is highly prized. In Trinidad and Peru their nesting places are raided and the young birds are taken and killed.

3/ How Does a Malleefowl Tell Temperature?

Most birds build nests. The robin uses twigs and grasses. The swallow makes a nest with mud and branches. The ovenbird of South America bakes a nest of clay. All of these birds sit on their eggs and keep them warm with the heat of their bodies. This helps the eggs to hatch, and it's called brooding.

But there's one bird that has a very different way of hatching eggs—the *malleefowl,* often called the *megapode* or *incubator bird.* This bird probably makes the oddest nest in the world.

The malleefowl starts its nest in June. First, the male and female birds scoop out a hole together in the sand. Then the male malleefowl rakes into it leaves, grass and whatever other vegetable material he can find. It's a lot of work for this chicken-sized bird to collect all that vegetation. But he keeps it up for weeks, until there is a mound of vegetable matter as much as fifteen feet high.

Meanwhile the sun has been shining on the mound. And rain has been falling on it. The combina-

tion of sun and water begins to rot the leaves and grass. As they rot, they produce heat. The mound is getting nice and warm!

About the beginning of August the pair of birds make a pit in the center of the mound. They line it with sand. In September the female lays the first egg in the pit. She lays one egg every three or four days until about thirty eggs are in the nest. During this time the male malleefowl never leaves his job, which is to keep the eggs at a constant temperature so they will hatch.

The male tests the mound about five times a day by pushing his beak into it. If it feels too hot, he opens the pile at the top and lets some of the heat out. If it's too cold, he throws sand or dirt on it to act as an extra "blanket" for the eggs.

How does this bird tell temperature? Ornithologists have discovered that the malleefowl's tongue is a very accurate thermometer. Tests have been made where heating coils were put into a malleefowl's nest, and the temperature of the mound was changed every few minutes. As fast as it was changed, the bird changed it back, even if he had to work on the mound constantly.

The malleefowl, which is distantly related to our American turkey, is found in Australia, New Guinea, Malaya, Samoa and the Philippines. In some of these countries, people harvest the eggs of the incubator bird the way we collect chickens' eggs.

4/ Why Are That Bird's Feet So Red?

Imagine a bird about the size of a pigeon that looks like a parrot. That's the *puffin.* It makes a comical picture as it waddles over the rocks in its bright "costume." Why is the puffin's beak so brightly colored? And why are its feet so red?

The answer is that the puffin is dressed for mating. When breeding time comes, the feet of both male and female turn red. And their beaks, which are usually yellow, become brightly striped. Even the little horny patches around their eyes change into colorful triangles.

All of these changes are signals to mark the beginning of the courtship season and to attract the attention of puffins of the opposite sex.

But once a puffin pair has mated and hatched one egg, the colorful time is over. Their feet and beaks turn a drab grayish yellow. Then the puffins leave their nests in the cliffs and return to the sea.

There are about fifteen million puffins in the world. Some of them live in the icy seas of the Arctic.

The Atlantic puffin shown here is found from north-west Greenland to the coast of Maine, as well as from Iceland to Portugal.

Puffins can fly, although when they first take off, it often looks as though they're not going to get off the ground. They are great swimmers, often "flying" under the water by using their wings.

5/   Is That a Bird on the Zebra's Back?

Who wants to sit on a zebra's back? The *oxpecker*, or *tickbird*. This little African bird spends most of its life in the company of large animals. Hippos, rhinoceros, oxen, zebras or gazelles can all be hosts to the tickbird, which treats them like its dinner table. It eats the ticks, flies and other small creatures that crawl on the animals. The oxpecker gets everything it needs from its animal host. It eats, sunbathes, mates on the back of its favorite animal. It may even take its nesting material from the hair on the animal's back!

Sometimes a dozen or more oxpeckers will settle on the back of a zebra. The zebra doesn't seem to mind its uninvited guests. Perhaps it is because the bird and the zebra each do something for the other. That's called symbiosis. The zebra supplies the tickbird with food. The tickbird takes care of the zebra's sores, slitting its skin like a skillful surgeon and cleaning out the wounds. And there's something else that the tickbird does. Hunters have noticed that when they try to sneak up on an animal with tickbirds

on it, the birds sense their presence and warn the animal. The oxpecker is perfectly suited for the life it leads. Its claws are made for climbing an animal's legs and for hanging on when the animal is running.

There are two kinds of oxpeckers—yellow-billed and red-billed. They are both related to starlings. One lives mainly in East Africa, the other throughout most of the rest of Africa, but occasionally their ranges overlap.

6/ Does the Bowerbird Know Beauty?

When spring comes, birds look for a mate. The male bird of each species has its own way of attracting a female. Male orioles sing a mating song. Geese do a special courtship dance. Birds that are colorful, like the male peacock, strut and show off their feathers. And the frigate bird blows his red throat pouch up like a balloon.

But there's one group of birds which has developed a most unusual way of showing off. The *bowerbirds* of New Guinea and Australia build a beautiful structure called a bower.

The male does the building. His bower may resemble a little thatch-roofed house. It may look like a small tunnel made of grasses. Or it may be like a maypole. Whatever way he does it, it is with great care. And he decorates it with flowers, berries, shells and whatever other shiny or colorful objects he can find. A chocolate wrapper or a bottle cap may find its way into a bowerbird's bower, if the bird is attracted to its color.

Many bowerbirds add a "garden" in front of the bower, and this too is carefully arranged with ferns, grasses and piles of colorful stones. Some species of bowerbirds even "paint" the insides of their bowers, holding a piece of bark in their beaks and dipping it in berry juice.

When the bower is finished, the bird stays near it, puttering about and adding fresh flowers as the older ones wilt and fade. Meanwhile, he sings, calling to a female bowerbird to come take a look at his handiwork.

When a female does appear, she will first peek through the bushes at the bower. The male stands in his garden and calls to her and bows. He does everything he can to get her to enter the bower.

If she does, the two birds will often mate there. Then the female will go off to build a nest somewhere else. The bower is never used as a nest; it is only a place for courting.

Why does the bowerbird go to so much trouble to build its bower? And why will it continue to work on the bower long after mating season is over? Some scientists now believe that this bird may actually have a sense of color and design and get pleasure from making something beautiful.

7/ Can a Bird Help a Fisherman?

In the rivers of China, Japan and India you often see a strange sight—fishing boats with several birds on them. If you look closer, you'll see that the birds have collars around their necks and leashes attached to the collars.

The birds are *cormorants*. And for hundreds of years Asian fishermen have used them to help catch fish. The cormorant is an excellent fisherman. It can dive deep into the water and stay under for a long time—long enough to find and catch a fish. Cormorants have been known to catch as many as 150 fish in an hour.

If the cormorant is fishing for itself, it swallows a fish as soon as it catches it. But the cormorant who works for a human doesn't get a chance to eat its catch. The leather collar around the bird's neck blocks its throat and keeps it from swallowing the fish. The fisherman gets the fish that the bird has worked for. The cormorant's reward is a few fish when the day's work is done.

Cormorants are always near water. There are several species that live in the United States and Canada. You may spy a group of them sitting, spaced evenly apart, on a pier or a small island, or even on a rock in the water. You can recognize the cormorant by its hooked beak and by its habit of sitting with its wings outstretched to dry.

8/ How Crazy Is a Cuckoo?

People say that to be crazy is to be "cuckoo." Certainly the *cuckoo* has some very odd habits. But it is also rather clever.

The common cuckoo is a parasite, which is an organism that lives off other individuals in some way. The cuckoo doesn't build its own nest, but lays its eggs in the nests of other birds. It depends on the other bird to feed and raise its young.

The cuckoo carefully picks the birds it wants for parents for its young ones. The common cuckoo of England, for example, often picks the European robin. It watches a nesting female robin closely for several days during the mating season. On the morning when the bird lays her first egg in the nest, the cuckoo is on guard. When the mama redbreast leaves the nest in the afternoon, the cuckoo goes down to the bird's nest, swallows or destroys the host's first egg and lays her own egg in the nest. Then she flies away. When the mother robin comes back, she sits on the egg, thinking that it is her own, and continues to lay the rest of her eggs.

The cuckoo lays an egg in a different "host" nest every few days, until she has about fifteen eggs scattered around in various nests.

Back at the nests, each mother bird is by now sitting on a batch of eggs, called a clutch. None of the birds knows that she is hatching a cuckoo egg along with her own. Now, in each nest the cuckoo egg hatches first, because it was laid first.

The cuckoo chick promptly puts its tiny shoulder against one after another of the other eggs and pushes them out of the nest.

Then it calls for food.

The female bird, thinking that one of her eggs has hatched, feeds it. And feeds it and feeds it and feeds it. Until one day the baby may be bigger than its foster parent! But even then she will continue to feed it, even if she has to climb on its back to fill that enormous mouth with her tiny beak!

Why doesn't the mother bird know that this young giant is not her offspring? The reason for that is very interesting.

First, a cuckoo may pick for a host a species of bird whose eggs match its own in size and color. And as if that weren't strange enough, the open mouth of the baby cuckoo is often the same color as the mouth of the host bird. When a bird parent looks into the open mouth, it thinks it is looking straight into the mouth of one of its own young.

Not all cuckoos lay their eggs in other bird's

nests, but the common cuckoo of Europe is famous for this behavior. In Hungary, its favorite target is the great reed warbler. Its greenish brown eggs are identical to those of the warbler.

9/ Can a Bird Use Tools?

The Galapagos Islands off the western coast of South America are unique in many ways. Only here will you see giant tortoises crawling over black lava rocks, or find gray marine iguanas splashing in the sea. And here you will find tiny sparrowlike birds that live nowhere else on earth. They are *Darwin's finches,* named after Charles Darwin, the English naturalist who first observed them.

When Charles Darwin studied the finches on the Galapagos, he noticed that they were not like the finches on the mainland of South America. They were even, in some cases, different from one another. Why? he asked himself. As usual, the answer to the question *why* was interesting. Darwin figured out that the ancestors of these birds had been blown from the mainland of South America in high winds. They had settled on the Galapagos. Over a very long period of time, their new way of life on the islands gradually began to change the appearance and habits of the finches. And depending on where they lived in the

islands, they even began to look different from one another. Charles Darwin saw that animal populations change depending on where they live and what they have to do to survive. He called it adaptation.

Now there are fourteen different species of Darwin's finches in the Galapagos Islands. Some eat seeds and some eat fruit. One of them, the *woodpecker finch*, eats insects. But how do you get insects out of trees if you don't have the strong beak and the long tongue of a woodpecker? That's the problem that this Darwin's finch had to solve in order for it to survive. It has solved it in a most remarkable way. This little bird uses a tool. When the woodpecker finch finds a hole with insects in it, it takes a sharp cactus spine or a twig and sticks it into the hole. It spears the bug, pulls it out of the hole, takes it off the twig and eats it. This species of Darwin's finch is a rare example of a bird successfully using a tool.

10/ If It's a Bird, Why Can't It Fly?

Not all birds fly. But the ones that can't usually get around very well some other way. Ostriches run fast. Penguins swim. But the *hoatzin* is another story. This South American jungle bird can barely flap its way from branch to branch. It seems, at first glance, like one of nature's mistakes—wings too long, feet like baseball mitts. And a body that's top-heavy. After a hoatzin has had a meal, its feet can't support it. It must lean its upper body against its perch to balance. In fact, the hoatzin is the only bird that has developed a horny pad on its chest for leaning!

Young hoatzins bear a striking resemblance to archaeopteryx (p. 12). Like that first bird, they have claws on their wings. They're used for climbing while the bird is small. But even with extra "hands," a young hoatzin is extremely clumsy.

What does a bird like the hoatzin do to protect itself? How can it survive if it can't fly or run from danger?

One thing the hoatzin has for protection is a

very bad odor. Few animals, including humans, want to eat it. In fact, its nickname among South Americans is "stinking Ana."

Another survival trait which the hoatzin has developed is its habit of diving into the water from a perch above a stream. This is rare behavior for a land bird and must be a trick the hoatzin has evolved for safety. Here's naturalist William Beebe's description of a young hoatzin threatened by a human climbing its tree:

> "The young hoatzin stood erect for an instant, and then both wings of the little bird were stretched loosely straight back, not folded bird-wise but dangling loosely and reaching well beyond the body. For a . . . time he leaned forward. Then without effort he dived straight downward, as beautifully as a seal . . . . very swiftly. There was a scarcely noticeable splash and . . . . I watched the widening ripples . . . over the muddy water—the only trace of the whereabouts of the young bird."

11/ Why Are Vultures Bald?

High in the sky above the California mountains flies a condor, the king of the vultures. It weighs about 25 pounds. Its open wings are 10 feet long, yet it seems to have no trouble staying in the air. It rides the air currents like a glider pilot, letting the warm air lift it as it glides and circles in its search for food.

Suddenly it sees a turkey vulture miles away. The bird is dropping toward the ground. The condor follows, because it knows the other vulture has found food.

Now all the vultures begin to gather. Something is dying or dead.

The condor is down on the ground. It sees a dying deer lying in the grass. And all around it, vultures. Waiting. They look like mourners at a deathbed. They have to be sure that the deer is dead. These small vultures are not strong enough to risk a kick from an animal that is still alive.

But the condor doesn't wait. He goes to the deer and begins to tear its flesh with his strong beak. The

other vultures let him have the choice parts. Then at last they move in to eat. More vultures come. Soon the grass and the deer are covered with them. By the time they are finished eating, only the animal's bones are left.

Looking at the condor, it is easy to tell that it is related to the other vultures. It has the same beak shape and the same naked head, bald of feathers.

Why are all vultures bald?

Because they spend a lot of time with their heads inside dead animals. If they had feathers on their heads, the feathers would get matted with blood and be hard to clean. They would be breeding places for germs. So the vultures, over long years of history, have evolved a "naked" head, open to the cleansing rain and sun.

Few people like vultures. They're not pretty birds, and they don't sing. They always seem to be around when a creature is dying. But in spite of their unpleasant habits, vultures have a very necessary place in the chain of life. If there were no condors and other vultures, imagine how many dead animals would lie in the open, breeding disease.

The California condor is the largest flying bird in the United States and is an endangered species. There are only about 40 left, and they are protected in a small range in the far west.

12/   Did That Bird Say Something?

Making sounds is a way birds keep in touch with other birds. An oriole singing in a tree in spring announces that the tree is his territory. A blue jay's screaming tells other jays that a cat is near. Different calls mean different things in bird language. Each species of bird has its own set of calls, as unmistakable as the bird's color. Except for the birds which are copycats!

The mockingbird, for instance, not only has a lovely song of its own, but it can imitate the call of as many as 55 other kinds of birds. Parrots and mynahs also are mimics.

But the most remarkable mimic in the bird world is the Australian *lyrebird*. Some bird experts say that no other bird comes close to it for the beauty and power of its song and for its ability to copy other sounds. One minute the lyrebird can sound like a chorus of cockatoos. The next minute it will mimic the song of a thrush. It can make a sound like a chair scraping, a dinner bell, a fire siren, and dozens of

45

other sounds. Once a lyrebird imitated so perfectly the alarm bell at a lumber camp that all the workmen came running to see where the accident was!

It's interesting to try to figure out why a bird in the wild would want to imitate a train whistle or some other "people sound." Can it be that the bird does it for fun?

Index